T0372181

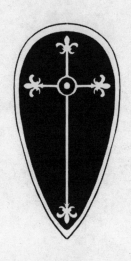

HOME SWEET CASTLE

There's no man like a Norman!

HORRIBLE HISTORIES®

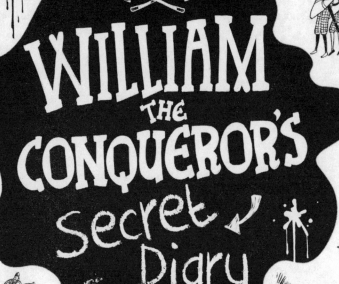

WILLIAM THE CONQUEROR'S secret Diary

CHARGE!

HANDS OFF!

Terry Deary

Illustrated by
Mike Phillips

SCHOLASTIC

Published in the UK by Scholastic, 2022
1 London Bridge, London, SE1 9BA
Scholastic Ireland, 89E Lagan Road, Dublin Industrial Estate, Glasnevin,
Dublin, D11 HP5F

Text © Terry Deary, 2022
Illustrations © Mike Phillips, 2022

ISBN 978 0702 31236 6

A CIP catalogue record for this book is available from the British Library.

Printed and bound in the UK by CPI Group (UK) Ltd, Croydon, CR0 4YY
Paper made from wood grown in sustainable forests and other controlled sources.

2 4 6 8 10 9 7 5 3 1

www.scholastic.co.uk

CONTENTS

1066 – Christmas and Crown   9

1066 – Riots and Wrongs   14

1034 – Monk and Mother   21

1035 – Dead Dukes   26

1035 – Blood on the Beaches   40

1035 – Harefoot Horror   53

1035 – Death and Glory   58

1042 – Edward Succeeds   66

1047 – Fighting for Life   70

1050 – Runaway Success   75

1050 – The Danger Years   81

1050 – Meeting Matilda   86

1051 – Marrying Matilda   95

1053 – Matilda's dreams   102

1064 – Harold Hostage   111

1066 – Edward's End   116

1066 – Family Feuding   123

1066 – Landing and Loss   127

1067 – Rebels and Revenge   137

1068 – Ending England   141

1077 – Family and Fall   146

1083 – Matilda Mourned   151

1087 – Regrets and Endings   153

That's ME!

WILLIAM

→

I'm a
CONQUEROR!

NORMANS
RULE
OK!

1066
CHRISTMAS AND CROWN

Ah, there you are, Miss Nun. Do you have a name, Miss Nun? Eva? What? Eva? Eve was the first woman in the world. Was that you? You look old enough. Hah! Just my little joke, Eva. Cruel? No. Don't ever call me cruel. Just honest. I mean, look at you. I may not be a great writer, but I can draw.

ASTRID

SISTER EVA

I have hunting dogs that are better-looking than you.

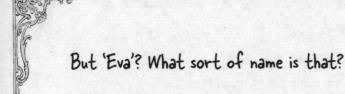

But 'Eva'? What sort of name is that?

French? Pah. I hate the French. No, I am NOT French. I am NORMAN. We live in the North of France — Normandy — but our blood is Viking. I am William, Duke of NORMANDY. What am I? That's right, and don't forget it. Of course, people CAN forget it because after the coronation today I am KING William the First of ENGLAND.

That can be the title of the book.

What do you mean, 'What book'? Didn't the top woman in your nunnery — ye-es, yes, the abbess woman — didn't the abbess tell you why you are here? You are HERE to gather my old diaries and tell my life story.

A thousand years from now, writers will tell the story of the greatest king ever to rule England — that's me, by the way — but I want to tell my own story. I want to make sure the readers in 2066 see 1066 from MY point of view.

I don't want history writers of the future making me look cruel, ruthless and bloodthirsty just because I had to do a few cruel, ruthless and bloodthirsty things. I'm not cruel.

Then you can hide our book in your nunnery library. It could be found a thousand years from now.

This pile of parchments — yes, the pile here on the table — these are the notes I made from time to time.

Put them in order. Like a diary. Of course,
I couldn't write when I was a baby. I am a
brilliant man, but no one is THAT brilliant.
So, before you start on my parchment pile,
I can give you the story before they begin.

You can start my story before I was born,
if you like. There's the story that my mother
had a dream. She dreamed a tree was growing
from her and the shade of the tree covered
Normandy and England. And, as you see, I now
cast my great shadow over Normandy and
England.

Poor old mother. A peasant — but don't write
that. She was the daughter of a tanner —
you know, the man that turns animal skins into

leather. A smelly job. Though another story says granddad had the charming job of preparing corpses for burial — tidying them up and dressing them.

I've made a lot of work for the corpse-dressers in my life. I've made a lot of corpses. Hah, just another of my little jokes.

Ah, can we stop there, Sister Eva? There's a knocking at my door and it sounds urgent. We'll go on tomorrow. You look at my old diaries. The king of England has troubles.

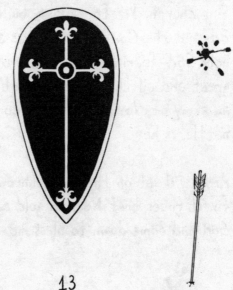

1066
RIOTS AND WRONGS

Panic, Sister Eva. That's all it was. When we were disturbed yesterday it was a messenger come to say, 'London is still burning. Help, oh helpy, helpy help.'

This is what happened: I went to Westminster Abbey to be crowned. It was a fine church, fit for a king, built by holy old Edward the Confessor. He was a real holy-holy God-fearing man. I mean to say, God is great and all that, but he's not as useful as an army of Normans when it comes to a battle, is he?

Anyway, I sat on the great throne in all the finest robes that Norman gold can buy. If God had come down to bless me — which he

didn't by the way — but if he did then I'd have made him look shabby.

(Sorry, Sister Eva, that is only a joke. I know you think I shouldn't joke about God. God is great, blah, blah.)

As I was saying, the crown was put on my head, the head where it belonged. And my lords and ladies looked at me in wonder. You would too if you'd been there.

Now, I wanted to be king of the Saxons — the beaten people of England. So, I was crowned by Archbishop Ealdred of York. But we also

threw in an old Norman custom — I had Bishop Geoffrey from France do the crowning all over again in the French language. He marked me with French holy oil.

The whole thing went on a bit, and I was getting hungry, but it was worth it. See? The English AND the French BOTH knew I was the rightful king.

I even invited some of the Saxon lords ... the ones I'd beaten. And that was what caused the problem. I'd put guards outside the church where the English peasants were waiting. They all wanted to catch a look at their handsome king — that's me.

Anyway, the order was simple. If any of the English did NOT show great joy, then the guards would give them the chop — and I don't mean a lamb chop. (That reminds me, Sister Eva, I was getting hungry by the end. I may have said that?)

16

The Norman lords cheered when it was all over. 'Vivat!' they cried. (That's Latin for 'Long may he live.') The Saxon lords shouted, 'God save the king.'

Between the two lots of lords and ladies, French and English, all that shouting was causing a right racket. Now my guards, bless them, thought there was a riot going on inside the church, so they did what they always do when there's danger. They rushed off and set fire to everything in sight.

IS IT THE 'RIOT-TIME' TO START BURNING?

It's a wonder they didn't set fire to me in the church. THAT would have been a coronation to remember, wouldn't it?

All right, Sister Eva, maybe God WAS there looking after me. One of your monk friends — a bloke called Orderic Vitalis — wrote a report. Copy it into my diary.

As the fire spread through the houses, the people who had been cheering in the church were thrown into a panic. A crowd of men and women rushed out of the church. Only the bishops and priests along with the monks stayed, terrified, in front of the altar. They only just managed to finish the coronation of William, who was pale and trembling.

Nearly everyone else ran towards the raging fire, some to fight bravely against the force of the flames and beat them out. Others were simply hoping to grab loot for themselves in the great confusion.

The English believe there is a Norman plot — a Norman excuse to rob the city — and are very angry. They say the Normans cannot be trusted.

Now, I want you to cut out that bit about me being pale and trembling. Of course, I've never 'paled' or 'trembled' in my life.

But I don't mind that bit about the Normans not being 'trusted'. I WANT the Saxon English to fear us.

If they do decide to rebel, I'll have a great castle built by the river — a Tower of London. My Norman architect has already done some plans.

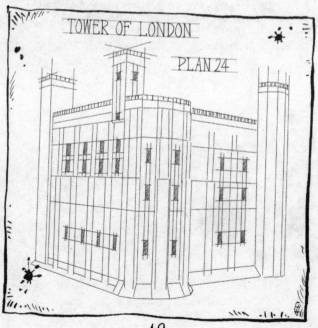

A fine palace for England's new king.

But now, Sister Eva, let us have the first pages of my secret diary. In those days I had a monk as a teacher, not a fine nun like you. He taught me to write. My lessons were so harsh I learned to hate writing. I suppose that's why you are doing it for me now.

But back to my old diary. It started when I was seven.

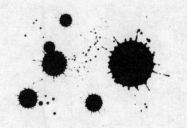

1034
MONK AND MOTHER

I learn to write. A monk is my teacher. He says that I must keep a diary. My father, Duke Robert, always said I must keep a diary. This is my diary. I am seven years old and very handsome.

ME! LOOKING
INCREDIBLY
HANDSOME!

I carry a small sword. When I grow up, I will carry a big sword and fight. I would rather fight than write. But today I must write.

I will write what I do and what I think. That is a diary. But I do not have time. I will write WHEN I have time.

Today I am doing nothing. All I am doing today is learning to write. This is my tenth try. I keep getting it wrong. I smudge my ink. I spell words bad. I forget full stops.

Brother Mundi is a monk. He teaches me to write. When I get writing wrong, he makes me start all over again. This is my tenth try. I am sorry. I have already said that.

I am William. I live in Normandy. Normandy is the land to the north of the country they call France. France is full of French people. I do not like French people. Brother Mundi is a French person. He says he is a NICE French person.

Brother Mundi has a rope belt.

BROTHER
MUNDI

If I do not write nice things about him, he
will beat me with his belt. Monks are kind and
gentle people. Brother Mundi is the most kind
and gentle monk in the world. When he beats
me he is kind and gentle.

I love Maman, even though she has gone off
to marry another man.

I will write this diary to please her. Maman
says she had a dream before I was born. In
her dream she did not give birth to baby

23

William. She gave birth to a huge tree. The tree cast a shadow over Normandy and the strange island across the sea called England.

Wise men say her dream is a sign. It is a sign that one day I shall cast a shadow over both lands. I shall rule them.

I shall be a good ruler. I shall be kind to all men, women and children. But maybe not monks. Maybe one monk will be flogged with a

rope, so he knows what it is like. Now I am
a lord, I may even do the beating myself.

Let's say the monk's name will be Sundi. Not
Mundi. That would be revenge. Brother Mundi
is kind and beats me gently with his rope belt,
as I said. Revenge is not nice. Neither is being
beaten with a rope.

1035
DEAD DUKES

Now Brother Mundi is making me draw a family tree. How can a family be a tree? But here's the best I can do.

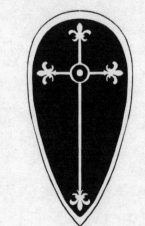

Bother Mundi has been teaching me about my past. I like these lessons. I did not know history could be such horrible fun. When I am Duke of Normandy I shall learn from the good dukes and not make the mistakes of the bad dukes. Here is what I learned.

ROLLO – GOOD GUY

I like Rollo. My great-great-great grandfather. He was a Viking but was thrown out of his lands because he had to fight everyone. He took his warriors south and settled in France, where he did lots of battering the local people.

ROLLO

At last he made peace with the French and was supposed to pay homage to the king of France for his land. The idea was that Rollo would kneel in front of the French king, Charles III. Rollo could do that.

He would place his hands together and let the

28

French king wrap his royal hands around Rollo's — that's to show his power. Rollo could do that.

THEN Rollo had to kiss the king's foot. Rollo could NOT do that. He said, 'I will never bow my knees at the knees of any man and kiss his foot.'

That caused a problem. A B-I-G problem. But Rollo solved it. I can just see it.

1. Rollo's told one of his warriors to kiss the French king's foot. The warrior knelt down in front of Charles III, who was standing up.
2. The warrior grabbed the king's foot and lifted it high.
3. The king fell over backwards, and everybody laughed.

Part of the peace deal was that Rollo would become a Christian. We Normans still are. That is why I have a Christian monk, Mundi, to teach me.

But when Rollo grew old, he went mad. He turned back to the old Viking gods and sacrificed a hundred Christians to them. Lopped off their heads. Lop, lop, loppity-lop. That must have been fun.

Sorry, Mundi, what I should have said was that was a wicked act and Rollo will burn in hell. It's not easy being a Norman duke. There are so many people who want to kill you. I will be in danger every hour when I become Duke William of Normandy.

I will just HAVE to be ruthless. Even the horrible bits of history can teach me.

Anyway, I was writing a history of my family. Who was the second Deadly Duke?

WILLIAM LONGSWORD –
FROM 927 TO 942

I learned THREE things from William Longsword's life.

● He started to act like a French lord and his Viking warriors hated that. In AD 933 they rebelled. First lesson: be a true and vicious Viking.

● The Viking rebels surrounded William and trapped him in the town of Rouen. They waited for him to give up or starve. What did he do? He rode out and smashed the rebel army. Second lesson: the best way to defend yourself is to attack.

● In AD 942 Longsword went to a meeting to make peace with his deadly enemy, Arnulf. Arnulf's men ambushed William and killed him. We have a jousting dummy in our castle. We charge it with a lance for practice.

CHARRRRGE!

DUMMY

That dummy doesn't have a lot of brains. But it has more than William Longsword. Third lesson: trust nobody, because as soon as you do, they will kill you.

RICHARD I, THE FEARLESS, THIRD DUKE OF NORMANDY — FROM 942 TO 996

This Richard was only ten years old when his dad Longsword was assassinated. Richard started one of those endless wars with the king of France and called his Viking friends to help.

I knew what would happen next, even before Mundi told me. Yes, dear diary, the Vikings from the icy north wanted to stay in lovely, rich Normandy. They were more trouble to Richard than the French enemies.

Now, Richard had a beautiful daughter, named Emma. 'Remember Emma,' Mundi told me. 'She will be very important.'

EMMA

Then Richard died after he'd been Duke for fifty-four years. Maybe I will be duke for sixty years. Or maybe – Mundi says – my enemies will kill me first.

RICHARD II, THE GOOD, FOURTH DUKE – FROM 996 TO 1026

Not a very exciting duke, if you ask me. (Sorry, Grandad.) He was known as Richard the Good. I mean how boring is that?

He gave lots of money to monasteries. The monks write the history books, so of COURSE they said he was 'Good'. They were paid to say that. Pah. When I am Duke of Normandy, you won't catch me giving money away to miserable, mouldy, mumbling monks, mate. I wonder what they'll call me? Will the Wonderfully Mean? I don't care.

Anyway, around the year 1000, an English king called Ethelred dared to invade Normandy. But our knights attacked his army so swiftly they knocked the evil English back into the Channel like dogs with their tails between their legs.

NEXT TIME I'LL BE READY!

I wish I'd been there. As soon as I'm twelve years old I will be.

England? A wet and wild country. But Richard II married off his sister – the beautiful Emma – to Ethelred and made her Queen of England.

Poor Emma had to go across the wetter and wilder English Channel to get there. Poor Great Aunt Emma.

LUNCH OVERBOARD!

BLAAH!

Then Ethelred was defeated by King Cnut and did the sensible thing and died. And who did Cnut force to marry him? Poor old Great

Aunt Emma. She was queen of England TWICE. ONCE would be bad enough.

Still, they do say that having Great Aunt Emma as queen of England means that one day I can claim to be king of England.

Would I want to be? Not really. Normandy is nicer. And drier.

Boring Richard II died in 1026 and even that was boring. He died of old age. Well, he was fifty-six years old.

He left Normandy to my uncle Richard.

RICHARD III, FIFTH DUKE – FROM 1026 TO 1027

Oh, Uncle Richard. You became duke but for the shortest time of any Norman lord. There was one person who killed you. Me.

Sorry, Uncle Richard, but my dad was your brother. If you died, Uncle Richard, my dad would be the sixth duke of Normandy. Then I was born.

Suddenly my dad had a son that HE could hand the throne to. Suddenly dad had a reason to want you dead. And that reason was me.

I was a wonderful baby, they say. When I was born my nurse said I grasped some straw from the bed and held it tight in my hand. So tight she couldn't take it off me.

'That is a sign the baby William will be a great ruler,' my mother cried. 'He will grab lands like he grabbed the straw.'

And then Uncle Richard died. He was at a feast where Robert and many of his knights fell sick and died.

People say that my dad paid Ralph Mowin to slip poison into the food at the feast. I asked him once, 'Dad? Did you poison Uncle Richard?'

Dad just threw back his head and laughed so hard I could see every one of his rotten teeth. 'Prove it, William. No one will ever prove it.'

ROBERT THE MAGNIFICENT, MY FATHER – FROM 1027 TO ?

So here I am. My father, Robert the Magnificent, is duke. And when he dies, I'll be duke.

Every day I train with an old soldier called Theroulde. He teaches me to ride and use the bow and arrow, the javelin, the sword and the spear. I have small suits of armour made for me.

ME, LOOKING FIERCE

Of course, I have to practise with someone, and I have a friend of my own age called Taillefer. I always beat him because I am so strong. But he smiles and is always ready to fight again.

Our teacher, Theroulde, says it's easy to win. It's braver to lose and keep fighting, so Taillefer is as brave as me.

I shall have to be a knight to fight for my Normandy. Taillefer says he shall be my minstrel and sing me into battle. He will be my jester and make my great lords happy when they visit. He says, 'I shall be your jongleur and amaze you with my juggling.'

There is talk of my father going to Jerusalem as a pilgrim. For my safety I have been sent to Paris. Good King Henry of France will protect me.

1035
BLOOD ON THE BEACHES

Theroulde told us all about our Viking past. And some of it was steeped in blood.

It seems that muddy kingdom of England was a battleground. The Saxons lived there when the Vikings invaded. Then the Saxons drove them out but the Vikings came back. 'Your great aunt Emma's first husband – King Ethelred of England – PAID the Vikings, filling their ships with gold, to leave him in peace.'

I remembered an old chronicle I'd read. The English people called the frightened king 'Ethelred the Unready'. I told Taillefer, 'If I'd been Ethelred, I would have taken my sword and driven the Vikings into the sea and

chopped them till the seas ran red. 'Ethelred the Unready Coward,' I sneered to my jongleur friend.

Theroulde snorted. 'Don't mock a brave king, young Will. A Viking called Cnut invaded England with a huge army of ten thousand Vikings.'

I love tales of battles. I like to draw them. I drew the Viking invasion.

'When Cnut's army landed, they attacked the poor English people. Ethelred fought back that time. Cnut fled with his army from the shores of England back to his home in Denmark.' Theroulde leaned forward and breathed. 'Cnut had English hostages – harmless men and women. Cnut cut off their ears and noses and scattered them on the shore before he left.'

I nodded. 'That's what I'd do. Cut bits off my hostages to teach the enemy a lesson.'

Taillefer agreed. 'Sometimes you have to be cruel to rule. Hey, Will,' he said, and his round face split in a grin. 'If someone cut off my nose, how would I smell?'

I sighed. 'I don't know, Taillefer. If someone cut off your nose, how would you smell?'

'I'd still smell terrible,' he laughed.

I groaned. His jokes are the worst in Normandy.

But I wanted to know more about Ethelred and Cnut and what happened to my great aunt Emma a dozen years before I was born.

Theroulde went on, 'Ethelred died and left your great aunt with two sons, Edward and Alfred.'

NAA-NA! BLAAH!

'Of course, one of the boys should have been king of England. But after Ethelred died, King Cnut returned.'

'Cutting off noses?' I asked.

'Who nose?' Taillefer joked.

Theroulde handed me a piece of parchment a monk had written. Taillefer looked over my shoulder as I read the chronicle.

Cnut was very tall and strong, and the most handsome of men, except for his nose, which was thin and a little hooked. He had fair skin and a fine, thick head of hair. His eyes were better than those of other people. They looked fine and gave him sharp sight.

We tried to picture this Viking King Cnut of England.

CNUT

Taillefer chuckled. 'Cnut would have to murder Edward and Alfred, wouldn't he?'

'Poor Emma,' I said. 'First her husband Ethelred died and then her two sons would die?'

Old Theroulde gave a sharp laugh. 'There is nothing poor about Emma. She saved BOTH of her sons.'

'She fought Cnut with a sword?' I asked.

Theroulde just shook his head. 'She did something much cleverer. She married Cnut. He couldn't murder his stepsons, could he?'

That was when a servant hammered on the door of the library we used as a school room. 'What is it?' I asked, annoyed that the gory story was not finished.

'Sire,' the servant gabbled, 'your aunt Emma has arrived in Paris to see your father.'

'He's in Palestine,' I said.

'Yes, sire,' the servant explained. 'YOU will have to greet her.'

And so, I will finally get to meet the queen of England, the queen of Denmark and the queen of Norway. I shall write more later.

LATER

Emma is awesome. Taillefer thinks he is a poet, and he has been going all poetic about my great aunt.

'She swept into the room like a hot wind from Africa. Her eyes burned fierce as flaming torches in a castle dungeon. Her voice was sharp as a Sica dagger, and the tapestries trembled when she spoke.'

UMMMMMM...

'Pfffft,' I snorted. 'She didn't scare me,' I lied.

'Then why was your voice shaking when you greeted her?' he laughed.

'I was cold,' I said. Taillefer just laughed.

But I remembered she was married to Cnut, the king who sliced off the ears and noses of his enemies. I will always remember her sitting on my father's throne as servants and soldiers cowered and quaked.

Great Aunt Emma spoke quickly. 'One of my sons, Edward or Alfred, will be the next king of England,' she said. 'One day YOU will be duke of Normandy.' She pointed a finger at me with a nail like a claw. 'You will be friends with the English. And — until he dies — your father will keep the peace with England. Understand?'

'Yes, ate grant Emma ... I mean Great Emma Aunt.'

49

She shook her head at the foolish boy who stood in front of her. 'When is your father back from Palestine?' she asked suddenly.

'I – erm – I um...'

Theroulde stepped forward and said quietly, 'He is on his way back from Jerusalem, your highness. He has been ill and has to be carried, so it will be a month or more before he is back.' He held out a map.

I'LL BE BACK IN A MONTH OR MORE

Queen Emma's face was sour. 'Ill? Serves him right. Only an idiot would go to the Holy Land.'

50

I gasped. I couldn't help myself. No one had ever called my father an idiot.

'Listen, sweet William,' she said with a smile as kind as a wolf. 'In the past the northern Vikings have invaded my English lands. Their ships have landed in Normandy, filled up with food and weapons, and made the short trip across the English Channel. They USED Normandy to help the attacks on my people.' The claw jabbed me in the shoulder. 'That will never happen again. You will not shelter the Viking enemies of England. Understand?'

'Yes, Aunt Gremma Ate.'

'Tell your father what I said. Remember?'

'Yes, Grant Ate.'

She rose from my father's throne. 'And never get it into your miserable little head that one day YOU could rule in England. My sons will rule and their sons after them.'

And she was gone. Trumpets sounded in the courtyard and banners flew as she rode down to the river and her waiting ship.

1035
HAREFOOT HORROR

Theroulde came to me this morning and his sun-browned face was pale. He carried a piece of parchment in his hand. 'Bad news, sire,' was all he said as he handed me the sheet to read.

Taillefer looked over my shoulder as I read the report, written in the hand of a monk. It told the grim tale of Great Aunt Emma's son – my half-cousin. Aunt Emma had two sons, Edward and Alfred. Now Cnut has died. That means one of her sons could be the next king of muddy, chilly England. Edward stayed in Normandy. Alfred crossed to England. To be a Norman king? The English hated the idea.

*A*lfred and his men landed and rode towards the town of Guildford in the south of England. The town is thirty miles south of London. They were met by the powerful Earl Godwin of Wessex. Godwin told Prince Alfred how loyal he was to him. He found the prince's troop of soldiers somewhere to rest for the night in the town.

The next morning, Godwin said to Alfred: 'I will go with you and watch you safely on your way to London. The great men of the kingdom are waiting for you. They want to make you their king.'

Godwin said this but he knew that Harold Harefoot had already taken the throne. Harold Harefoot was the son of King Cnut and his first wife. Godwin planned to lead Prince Alfred to his death.

Then Godwin took the prince and his men over the hill of Guildown, but that is on the road to Winchester, not London. Maybe

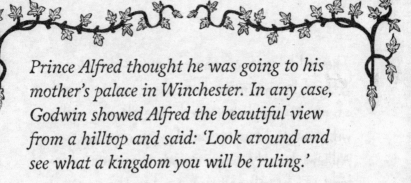

Prince Alfred thought he was going to his mother's palace in Winchester. In any case, Godwin showed Alfred the beautiful view from a hilltop and said: 'Look around and see what a kingdom you will be ruling.'

Alfred then gave thanks to God and promised that when he was crowned king, he would rule in a way that would please both God and the English people. At that moment, however, he was seized and tied up together with all his men. Nine-tenths of them were then murdered. There were still so many, the survivors were mostly killed. Alfred was tied to a horse and then carried by boat to a monastery at Ely. As the boat reached land, Alfred's eyes were put out. For a while he was cared for by the monks, who were fond of him. But soon after he died from his wounds.

'Poor Great Aunt Emma,' I said. 'She lost a son in that dreadful way.'

Theroulde spat on the rushes on the floor. 'Stupid Emma, more like.' He stood in front of me, his wind-browned face glowing red with anger. 'Two lessons for you, young William. Firstly, never trust the word of a lord. They will tell you any lies they want to steal power. Emma is lucky her other son, Edward, stayed back in Normandy.'

Taillefer looked up with a grin. 'What's the other lesson, oh wise old man?'

Theroulde bared his yellowed teeth and leaned closer. 'If you have to kill an enemy then do it in a cruel way like Godwin did. Don't just chop them. Torture them and make them suffer.'

'But why?' I cried.

'Because you want people to FEAR you. If a rebel thinks they will be executed they will take the risk. But if they think they will have their hands and feet, or noses and ears

cut off, they will think again.'

'Like Cnut did to his prisoners,' Tally muttered.

'Exactly,' Theroulde said with a nod.

'So that's THREE lessons, Will,' Tally said.
'Tell lies, trust nobody and be cruel.'

'Is there another way?' I asked with a shudder.

Theroulde gave a laugh like the bark of a dog.
'Yes, William. When you become duke, you can
simply let your enemies kill you.'

'I hope it will be a long time before I become
duke,' I said. 'I hope my father lives a long
time. Till I am grown enough to fight,' I said.

Theroulde spat again. 'Eyeless Alfred was
thirty years old when they blinded him. Being
a man doesn't save you. Only being clever.'

'And cruel,' Tally added.

1035
DEATH AND GLORY

Taillefer came to me this morning. I was still in bed. My friend fell to his knees and bowed his head. 'My lord,' he said.

I laughed. 'Is this one of your jokes, Tally?' I asked.

He looked up and for once there was no laughter in his eyes. 'No, my lord. You are duke of Normandy.'

'My father...'

'Is dead,' he said quietly. And a thousand thoughts raced through my head as Tally told the tale.

A messenger had arrived from Rome on a weary, dusty horse to bring the news.

They say my father had his brother – my Uncle Richard – poisoned. That was a sin. So, he decided to go to Jerusalem as pilgrim to the Holy Land to say sorry to God. Maybe he thought that would get him into heaven. I don't know. I only know I watched him go dressed as a humble pilgrim.

He may have looked like a pilgrim, but he was well fed and comfortable and had a small army of guards and servants.

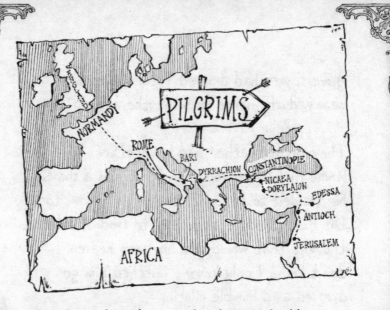

When he entered a great city, a city like Rome, he threw off the pilgrim act and paraded as a great lord.

At Constantinople, he showed off his wealth and glory. When he entered the city of Constantinople, he rode a mule. As well as being richly dressed, the mule had shoes of gold instead of iron.

He rode with banners flying and trumpets blaring. The golden shoes of the mule were fastened to the hoofs with short nails, so they were shaken off as the animal walked along. The poor people of Constantinople scrambled to pick them up and cheered the mighty duke of Normandy.

'He was showing off,' Taillefer said. 'The people of the city were dazzled by him. But God wasn't. Duke Robert reached Jerusalem but fell ill with a fever of the East. He was carried by slaves. And that was how he died.'

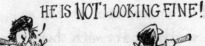

'All his wealth and all his power. He didn't die in battle like a hero. He was brought down by a little fever,' I said.

Taillefer looked at me with those sharp and clever eyes. 'He died of pride,' he said. 'You will be a great duke,' he went on. 'A great warrior. But never be too proud.'

I jumped from my bed, snatched the dagger from under my pillow and held it to his throat. 'How dare you insult Robert the Magnificent,' I shouted.

Taillefer shrugged and smiled. 'Just telling the truth,' he said quietly and pushed the point of the dagger away with a finger. 'Now you are duke there will be lords lapping at your feet, lying about how great you and your father are. They are waiting for you to turn your back. That is when they will stab you.'

He suddenly reached forward, twisted my wrist and sent my dagger spinning into the air. He caught it in his other hand, and it was at my throat. 'What you need, Will, is a friend who will tell you the truth — even the hard and painful truth. Every great household has one.'

I swallowed as I felt the prick of the dagger. 'Yes. They are called jesters.'

Tally nodded slowly. 'They entertain guests at feasts with their juggling and singing.'

He threw the dagger into the air, pulled out his own and kept the two knives whirring through the air fast as a pheasant's wing. I'd never seen juggling like it. My scowl turned to a smile.

'My first command as duke of Normandy is to make you my court jester ... my jongleur and my minstrel.'

Tally bowed low and said, 'I accept, your grace.'

Then he sang my favourite story. The tale of the knight Roland. And my favourite lines.

Roland blows his battle horn,
Drives his weary army on.
Roland blows his battle horn,
Till his great head bursts forth with blood.

At that moment there was a hammering on the door, and without waiting for an answer, old Theroulde burst in and gave a quick bow. 'Your grace,' he panted, 'news of your father's death has reached the whole country. Your knights are gathering armies to fight for the right to be duke.'

I was baffled. 'They all swore to my father they would make ME duke if anything happened to him,' I cried.

'Words, words, words, your grace. They only swore that out of fear of your father. Now he's dead they will fight for Normandy. That's why he sent you to be safe here in Paris.'

'And what will happen to me?'

Theroulde looked at the floor and muttered. 'The rebels all think the same thing. It will be best for them if you end up dead.'

It wasn't the best start to the first day of my rule, dear diary.

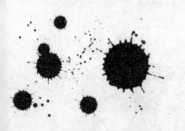

1042
EDWARD SUCCEEDS

Today I found this diary again after maybe five years. I had more important things to think about. Like staying alive.

Brother Mundi the monk started me writing this diary. But he soon fled back to his monastery when the rebels came to kill me. I don't blame him. He's a praying man not a slaying man.

I have been protected by the lords who served my father. They fought the lords who betrayed my father. And many died. At first, my greatest helper was Henry, king of France.

KING HENRY
OF FRANCE

But guarding me is dangerous. So many died trying to protect me. I was just twelve years old when the deaths started.

● Duke Alan of Brittany was my father's trusted cousin who cared for me. He fought against Herbert 'Wake-Dog'. He was called wake-dog because he had so many enemies he hardly dared to sleep. I know how he felt. Still, Alan had Herbert murdered. Then good Uncle Alan was attacking a rebel castle when he died. Suddenly. Poison, they say.

● Gilbert of Brionne took charge. Gilbert only lasted another few months. Gilbert went out for a peaceful ride. Two of my enemies set upon him and hacked him to death.

OOOPS!

● Turchetil, a cousin and a true friend was murdered.

● Osbern became my servant and slept outside my bedroom to keep me safe. That was deadly. One night assassins raced through the castle. Osbern stood in the way till help came. By the time Theroulde rescued me Osbern's throat had been cut.

● Walter stayed in my room most nights. One evening we were warned a small army was coming to kill me. We didn't have enough guards to hold them off. Walter took me into the village near my castle and dressed me as a peasant. When the enemies searched, they thought I was a peasant boy, and my life was saved.

That was when I moved back to France and King Henry gave me shelter there. Henry still made me bow before him.

Then, at last, I went home to Normandy.

I have a fine castle at Tallieres on the border with France. Today I had some strange news.

I have told how Emma's son Prince Alfred had been blinded on the orders of Harold Harefoot in England. Now Emma's other son, Edward, has taken the throne of England. He is a God-loving man and always telling God he confesses his sins. They call him Edward the Confessor. But he has no children. Who will take his throne when he dies?

Maybe one day I could be the next king after Cousin Edward?

All I need to do is stay alive.

1047
FIGHTING FOR LIFE

I survive. I am nineteen years old. Theroulde and Taillefer are the only ones I trust. Theroulde makes me strong, Taillefer makes me laugh. I do not need any other friends.

Even Henry of France has grown greedy and tried to steal my lands. I hate the French. I had a castle at Tallieres. Henry said it was too close to the border. He said my soldiers were attacking France and going to Tallieres to shelter.

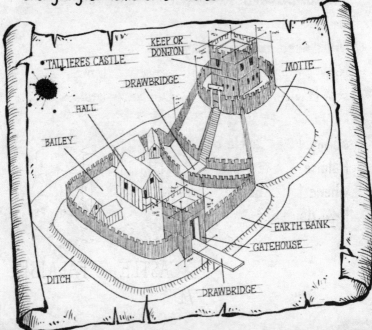

TALLIERES CASTLE

KEEP OR DONJON

DRAWBRIDGE

MOTTE

HALL

BAILEY

EARTH BANK

GATEHOUSE

DITCH

DRAWBRIDGE

Wicked Henry forced my troops to flatten Tallieres Castle until there wasn't a wooden wall standing.

OF ALL THE ROTTEN LUCK, A SPLINTER!

My true and loyal knights hated that. But Theroulde said, 'Revenge can wait.' And so, we waited.

Now the wait has ended. The vile Henry started attacking my castles and stealing my lands. At last, he arrived at my fine Castle of Falaise – the place where I was born. How dare he?

CASTLE OF FALAISE

71

The foul French troops formed a ring around the walls. Falaise Castle was too strong for Henry's men to break in. What did the coward do?

Theroulde told me, 'My spies say our castle commander is being paid gold to surrender without a fight. I need to lead a troop of knights and archers to drive off Henry's army and save the castle.'

'No, that is not your job,' I said. 'I will lead a troop of knights.'

Theroulde tried to argue but dear Tally said he would ride by my side and be my bodyguard. At last, Theroulde agreed but said he would ride at my other side. And so, we gathered our troops and their cheers shook the clouds when they saw me ride out to lead them.

I wasn't afraid of dying. My childhood had been so scary. I was always in danger of being murdered by people who wanted my land.

72

Henry is a good king, but I am a great warrior.
All of his army were FACING Falaise Castle.

Can you SEE how weak that is? I led my little
army and hit them from behind. They were so
shocked they began to run all the way back
to France. My people in Falaise castle cheered
as I entered the gates and set them free.
'William the Conqueror!' they cried. I like
that name.

The commander of the castle was my prisoner
now. I could have had him executed very
slowly. But my mood was so happy I set him
free. I won't always be so kind. I won't,
I swear.

1050
RUNAWAY SUCCESS

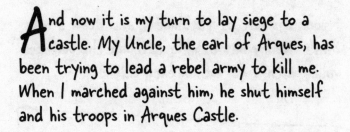

And now it is my turn to lay siege to a castle. My Uncle, the earl of Arques, has been trying to lead a rebel army to kill me. When I marched against him, he shut himself and his troops in Arques Castle.

We surrounded it. Then Theroulde brought me the news, 'King Henry of France is marching to help your enemy.'

'Remember Falaise,' Taillefer mumbled. 'If you surround a castle you must watch your back.'

I laughed. 'I will do better than that. I won't sit outside Arques Castle and wait to be attacked by Henry of France. I'll ride out to meet his army.'

Theroulde sucked air through his rotting yellow teeth. 'They are too powerful. They have knights in armour with lances to lead their charge with their battleaxes and pikes. They have hundreds of men behind them to cut us up when we fall.'

I took a sheet of parchment and drew a map on it. 'Henry has to ride through this narrow valley with a forest on each side.'

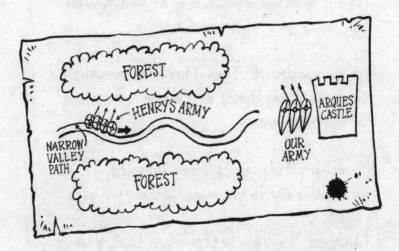

'We can hide half our men in that dark and gloomy forest,' Taillefer said. 'We will ambush them from both sides.'

I nodded. 'We will,' I agreed. 'But first we separate their knights and kill them off.'

'Their foot soldiers are right behind them,' Theroulde groaned.

'No, they're not,' I said. 'Right behind the knights are their servants. The cooks and squires with food and tents, the blacksmiths and the armourers, the weapon-makers and the horse grooms. They will have a line of slow wagons that block that narrow road. The foot soldiers come at the back. Look...' I drew again.

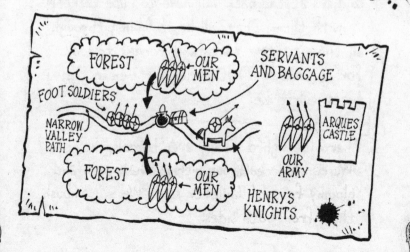

I tapped the plan. 'His knights will be at the front in all their glittering armour.'

Theroulde thumped his fist on the table. 'Henry's knights will see us. They will stop. They will make sure they are well fed and armed from the supply wagons while the foot soldiers make their way through to the front. They will be looking for an ambush, so they will be careful.'

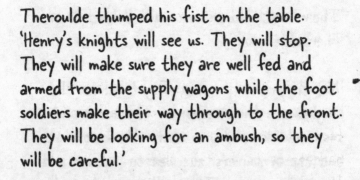

'Exactly,' I said and clapped my hands. 'So, we have to make them careless. We have to get those knights to charge forwards. The foot soldiers at the back will have to race to keep up with them. They will be stumbling through all those baggage carts and forget to look for an ambush. That's when our men in the trees will strike.'

Theroulde sighed. 'They aren't fools,' he argued. 'How do we make them rush out to attack?'

Taillefer threw back his head and laughed. 'We run away,' he cried.

'We run away,' I said with a smile. 'At least, we pretend to.'

'When the knights see us escaping, they'll charge out of the shelter of the forest. The foot soldiers will try to join them, and the baggage carts won't be able to get out of the way quickly enough. In all the tangle our men in the woods will strike with a storm of arrows and javelins and spears. Perfect.'

And so it was. Henry's knights charged at us. We stopped their horses with caltrops – spikes that cut through the feet of horses.

CALTROP

Don't feel sorry for the horses. They were French horses. The knights drew to a halt but there were no foot soldiers to follow up and join their attack. They were trapped behind the baggage carts and fighting for their lives against our attackers from the dark and dismal forest.

A French knight was faced by ten men with long, sharp pikes.

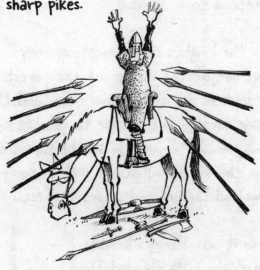

They threw down their weapons. They knew they were beaten.

It was my first great victory and taught me two lessons. Don't wait to be attacked but strike first. And pretending to run makes the enemy careless. I shall remember those lessons.

1050s
THE DANGER YEARS

Again, I have set my diary aside for years. I have no monk to tell me to write each day. Living with me meant danger, so Mundi fled back to his monastery again to pray.

I faced so many plots from lords who wanted me dead and Normandy for themselves. I could beat them in open battle. A history writer wrote this chronicle, and I kept a copy. See what he said about my battle at Val-ès-Dunes?

William was not scared at the sight of the enemy swords. He hurled himself at the enemies and terrified them with slaughter. Some of the enemy met their death on the field of battle, some were crushed and trampled in their rush to flee—a lot of enemy horsemen were drowned as they tried to escape across the river.

Served them right. But I wasn't cruel — it was just war.

They couldn't beat me in battle, so they tried to kill me in my bed. Taillefer arrived one night as I slept at Valonges.

'I saw a force gathering in Bayeux, Will — I mean, my lord. They are heading this way to kill you while your army is back at Falaise.'

I am ashamed. I didn't believe him. Good, true Taillefer. I dressed slowly and found a horse in the stables. I rode out with my friend and that is when I heard the sound of galloping horses and the jangle of armour. Tally had told the truth.

We fled to the woods and looked back at Valonges. My enemy was led by my own uncle — Guy — who claimed to be lord of Normandy.

We hid in the trees as they rode past in search of me. Hah. Fools. Useless, evil fools.

We took the secret roads though the midnight forest, starving and exhausted till we reached the safety of Falaise.

I am sorry, Taillefer. I will never doubt you again

I began by saying I wasn't cruel. Alencon, you say? All right. Some people say I was a bit cruel at Alencon.

Let me tell you my side of the story. I had to attack the town of Alencon because it was the home of a rebel force. They rode out to do battle and I drove them back behind the town walls. They escaped inside and a siege began.

I invited them to surrender. I was quite prepared to be merciful BUT they lined the walls and shouted insults. What insults you're asking? They made fun of my mother's peasant leather-working family. They dangled leather cowhides over a town wall. They shouted, 'Leather! Leather for the leather-worker's grandson!'

Of course, I captured prisoners when my men attacked. I paraded them in front of the townsfolk as they looked down from the town walls. Then I had their hands and feet cut off as their friends watched.

'Let them run away from me with no feet,' I snarled at Tally. 'Let them beat cowhides with no hands.' As they lay bleeding to death it was my turn to mock them. I placed the mangled bodies in a catapult and fired them over the walls, back to where they came from.

KEEP BOTH HANDS INSIDE THE BOWL AT ALL TIMES!

Not cruel. A fair punishment.

NO ONE INSULTS MY MOTHER.
NO ONE. UNDERSTAND?

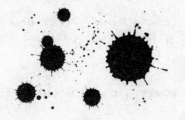

1050
MEETING MATILDA

One morning — about a month ago —
Taillefer came to me and said, 'I know why
so many lords want to murder you.'

'They are jealous of my power and my good
looks,' I said. 'I know that.'

'Yes, your power. No one would be jealous of
your looks.'

'What?' I snapped.

'A joke, my lord. You pay me to tell jokes.'

'I pay you to tell good jokes. Not insult me.'

'Calm down. Learn to laugh at yourself. I do.'

'You laugh at yourself?' I asked.

'No. I laugh at you,' he said with a grin.

He went on quickly before I had a chance to have him whipped. 'But there's another reason why so many want to murder you. It's because if you die, you have no son to take over. If you had sons, then they'd have to kill you AND your children to get your power. Not just you.'

He was right, of course. I was NOT going to tell him how wise he was. I just asked, 'As well as telling me to get a wife, maybe you'd like to tell me who the lucky lady is?'

He pretended to think about it. He looked across the cheese on the breakfast table and caught the eye of Theroulde. A little signal seemed to flash between them.

'She would have to be a princess,' Tally said, still pretending to think hard. 'Do you know any princesses – beautiful and the right age for William?' he asked. Theroulde gave a shrug, 'There's the Count of Flanders' daughter, Matilda.'

Tally threw back his head and laughed. 'The Count of Flanders MAY be a count, but he rules Flanders like a king. He has a strong army, and he has claims to the throne of England. The Count of Flanders? Hah. He would never let Matilda marry Duke William here.'

'Never,' Theroulde agreed with a sigh.

From that moment I knew I had to prove Tally and Theroulde wrong. I would marry Matilda or no one. Yes, dear diary, it's easy to look back and see that Theroulde and Tally tricked me into it. I can only say their trick worked. I sent messengers to the Count of Flanders and asked if we could talk about my marrying his daughter.

His messenger arrived and the letter said, 'Yes.' I was shocked. Tally and Theroulde smirked. That's when I knew it was THEIR plan, not mine. Great Aunt Emma married to make herself more powerful. I have decided that this is what I need to do.

We set off for Flanders to the north.

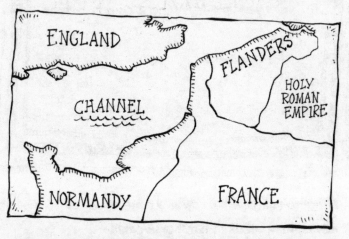

The servants at the count's castle showed me into the great hall where the walls were decorated with tapestries, all sewn in brilliant colours. A servant muttered quietly, 'Mistress Matilda made most of these. Isn't she a wonder with the needle?'

And the scenes from Flanders were amazing.
The man with the plough looked just like one
of my lumpen peasants.

A horse pulled a harrow in front of a
man sowing seeds. That horse could
have stepped straight from my stables.

ON YOUR HORSE!

The doors to the great hall swung open
and a lady appeared with a small and
pretty maid trotting behind her. The lady's
face was fierce and proud as a peacock.

'William of Normandy?' she asked. Her voice was harsh as a peacock screech too. 'My lady Matilda does not wish to marry you. You are too lowly for her. The grandson of a tanner cannot marry a princess.'

She turned on her heel and marched out. The tiny maid waited a moment, looked at me shyly and followed.

'Wait,' I called, but they were gone. There was nothing left for me to do but ride back to Normandy in a rage. My horse was saddled and Taillefer rode behind me, silent at my shame.

As I turned from the castle into the town outside its walls, I saw the small figure of the maid walking through the market. I jumped from my horse and ran after her. I grabbed her roughly by the shoulders, swung her round and shook her.

I thought I'd see fear in her face. Instead, I saw rage. 'How dare you handle a princess in that way?' she shouted.

I stepped back. 'A princess? You're Matilda's maid,' I laughed.

She looked up at me with eyes of fire. 'That was a little game we played. I wanted to see how much I liked your looks before I gave an answer.'

'What?' I shouted back. 'I am the one who decides, not you.' A crowd was gathering and watching us argue.

'I am a princess, you are the son of a peasant,' she spat. 'I choose.'

'I am a great warrior and I choose,' I told her.

'My father will decide, and he will decide what I tell him,' she said with a smirk as cruel as Taillefer's.

'So, tell your father the answer is yes,' I said, trying to stay calm.

She placed a finger on her chin and tilted her

head to one side. 'You are handsome enough,' she said. 'But a man who shakes a poor maid in that way is a coward.'

My mouth fell open. No one had ever dared to call me coward to my face. Taillefer spoke for me. 'She is right, Duke William,' he said. 'A knight is a gentleman. A knight does not raise a hand to a lady. He does not even raise his voice.'

'Taillefer,' I wailed. 'Why are you taking her side?'

'Someone has to,' Theroulde said.

I groaned. 'You too? Both of you. Traitors.'

Matilda raised her beautiful face and smiled. 'Friends,' she said. 'Friends are not afraid to tell their friends the truth. Even a truth you don't want to hear.'

I sighed. 'Princess Matilda, I am a humble duke of Normandy. Would you do me the honour of becoming my wife?'

She tilted her head to one side again like a sparrow. 'Very well, Duke William. I shall do you that honour. You may be a peasant woman's son, but I shall treat you as my equal.' The crowd who had gathered round us cheered and clapped their princess. The traitors Theroulde and Taillefer joined in.

And so, I shall have myself a wife.

I'M MARRYING MATILDA!

1051
MARRYING MATILDA

I am a warrior. I am happy when I am riding out with my armed men. We travel round Normandy to remind my people I am their lord. Any lords or peasants who want to rebel may think again when they see my power.

Matilda has made a wonderful tapestry of my troop riding out. She is clever with her fingers and needles and thread.

WILLIAM AND HIS CHUMS ON A DAY OUT...

As I say, I am a warrior. But Matilda says I should keep a record of our wedding. When Matilda orders, I obey.

Matilda arrived at my castle at Augi in a great parade with her parents, servants and friends. The knights and ladies rode on horses dressed as beautifully as the riders. Her knights were all glittering in armour of steel, to escort her.

BEST FEET FORWARD!

They moved across the country like a little army on a march. The wedding party went on for many days. Matilda wore a cloak studded with the richest jewels.

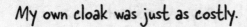

My own cloak was just as costly.

After the wedding we went to the great city of Rouen, where we lived with all the richness my bride could wish for.

Maybe not everything. She was a wonder with the needle and said the tapestries at Rouen were shabby and ugly. She brought her sewing maids from Flanders to help make new ones to line the walls with colour and keep out the drafts.

Theroulde grumbled, 'I'll swear she has more tapestry workers than you have knights, Duke William.'

Taillefer was happy enough as one of Matilda's ladies took his fancy. Her name was Adela. 'But you don't speak her language,' I teased him.

He shrugged and said, 'We speak through our eyes.' Then he made a mistake that almost

cost him his life. 'Anyway, a silent woman is the best sort.' My dearest wife heard that and flew into a rage. She wanted Tally whipped for his cheek and then hanged after his foul tongue had been cut out.

'It is a jester's right to say what he thinks,' I said.

'Let's see what he says when his tongue is thrown on the log fire in the great hall,' my duchess spat.

At last, we agreed Tally will be banned from the warmth and pleasures of the great hall to slave in the kitchens for a month.

Matilda brought her dogs too. I have hunting dogs, of course, but Matilda's were lap dogs. 'Pets' she called them.

SLURP!
SLURP!
SLOBBER!

98

I do not understand what use a dog is if it doesn't hunt or guard, but Matilda is mistress of the house, and she will have her way.

Last evening we finished a feast of wild boar that I had hunted that day and with rabbits that Matilda had brought down with her arrows. Some of my knights ate lampreys, a slimy, jawless eel with a single nose hole on top. This is not a fish loved for its good looks.

uck!

Matilda had brought to Rouen (along with her ladies) some lessons in good manners. They were posted on the door to the great hall for my knights to read and moan about.

Table Manners of Lords

1. Do not put your elbows on the table.
2. Do not lick your fingers.
3. Do not speak with your mouth full.
4. If you must belch, you should look up to the roof.
5. You must never spit over the table but behind you or into a cloth. Never spit like a peasant or eat like a ploughman.

Our feast was fit for a princess, which of course Matilda is.

There were other rules from royal Flanders nailed to the stables.

RULES FOR KNIGHTS

- Do not attack your enemy while he is squatting on the toilet.

- Do not mount your horse in the hall.

- Loosen your reins when riding over a bridge.

- If you eat at the table of the rich, then speak little.

Matilda said that I must obey those rules and set an example to my rough warrior knights. I obeyed.

My wife and I sat by the glowing embers of the fire and supped the last of the wine when we were alone at last. I looked at Matilda's handsome and proud face and spoke softly. 'I have given you riches and jewels, horses and servants, castles and lands. Is there a special gift I could give you to celebrate our marriage?'

She gave a half-smile and her eyes glittered in the red glow of the embers. She said just one word in answer. 'England.'

What Matilda wants I must provide. England must be ours. 'England? But not tonight, my love.'

Her smile grew wide and bright. 'Not tonight, Will,' she shrugged. 'Tomorrow will do.'

1053
MATILDA'S DREAMS

Matilda is a duchess. She was a princess. She wants to be a queen. England should be mine. Emma's son Edward is king. He wears the crown and sits on the throne – but everyone knows it is Lord Godwin and his armies that really rule.

I could build ships and cross the English Channel. But Godwin has the people of England behind him. Not any longer. This year it has begun to change and England's crown – Matilda's dream – is closer.

And now we have a fine son, Robert, named after my father Robert the Magnificent. We have another child on the way. If it is a man-child he shall be named Richard after my uncle. One shall rule Normandy and the other shall rule England. Matilda has decided.

But, first, Edward the English king must die.

'We can wait,' Matilda says.

Then, early in the year, a messenger brought a letter from King Edward of England. Taillefer read it. (He has been forgiven by me but not by Matilda.)

Westminster Palace

February in the year of Our Lord 1053

Dearest Cousin William,

I am sure you have heard the news from England. My Mother, your great aunt Emma, has died. Her last wishes were that I name you as ruler of England when I die. I cannot do that.
As you know the greatest earls of England must choose the next King. But I shall tell them you are my choice.

The son of Earl Godwin - Harold Godwinson - thinks he will be next King, but he is a violent and godless man. I pray every day that he may die before I do. England needs you and your fine wife, not some brutal soldier like Harold.

I shall pray for you and your family, dear cousin.

Edward
Rex

Matilda nodded wisely. 'I think you will have to kill this Harold Godwinson,' she said. 'Have him murdered or meet him in battle. But Harold must die.'

I shed a tear for Great Aunt Emma. A tear that only Taillefer saw. A great and wise woman. She was England's queen when she married Ethelred, and when Ethelred died, she married his greatest enemy, Cnut, and became queen again. Two of her sons had been kings of England. Alfred had his eyes put out and now her other son, Edward, took the throne.

'Edward is a liar,' Matilda raged at me. 'He hated his mother. He blamed her for marrying Cnut, he blamed her for Alfred's death. He packed her off to a convent to live like a prisoner with the nuns. A prisoner. A great queen who ended her life in poverty and misery. THAT is the truth.'

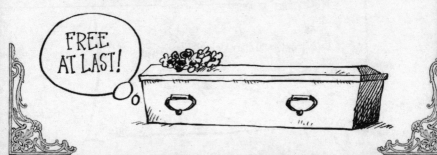

FREE AT LAST!

I nodded. 'Emma fought for power and lost in the end. But just think, Matilda, she will be in heaven and cheering for me to take the throne where she ruled for so long. As soon as godly Edward dies.'

'Then I hope she tells God to kill Edward,' my wife hissed.

But this year it was not Edward who died. It was others here in Normandy.

The first were two ladies from our palace. They were pretty and young, and I may have enjoyed walking and talking with them. Matilda was furious. Jealous.

I WONDER WHO LADY MATILDA KEEPS POINTING AT?

Matilda made me send them away and Tally took them to be nuns at Caen. But within a month they were both dead.

Wicked tongues said that Matilda had them poisoned. All lies, of course. My wife is fierce and may be jealous, but she would not murder two harmless young women. No, no. Never. I am sure she wouldn't.

We are surrounded by gossips who want to make trouble. But some stories are true. My loyal Theroulde came to me one morning and said there was money missing from our treasure chests. They held all of Matilda's jewels as well as the silver and gold we used to pay our soldiers.

'The thief has been clever,' Theroulde said. 'He has only taken a little every week and hoped that no one would notice.'

Theroulde is too old to ride out with our army now, so I have made him keeper of our castle. It is a job he does as heroically as when he fought at my side. Taillefer came into the room and added, 'I have checked the barracks. The knight Sampson of Rouen has a rich new sword and battleaxe with silver decorations on the handles. Far too fine for a common knight.'

Sampson was brought to me and knelt before me.

MY HOARD,
MY LORD,
MY SWORD!

He babbled like my baby son. 'My lord,' he squawked, 'I only took some treasure because Lady Matilda asked me to. She said that she wanted to flee back to Flanders, and we would live there together. She loves me.'

For a moment my breath left me. Matilda? Running back home? My wife and I argued every day — sometimes we screamed and shouted. We were bad-tempered people, I know, but she would never leave me. I began to wonder: would she murder two ladies in a nunnery? I suddenly thought I didn't know my wife.

I breathed again. 'Lock Sampson in a dungeon till I have tested his story,' I said calmly to Theroulde.

'Taillefer. Quickly find a monk, strip his robes off him and fetch them to me. Every day at noon Matilda goes to church to confess her sins to the priest. Today she shall confess to me.'

And so, I acted out my plan. I dressed as a monk, my true face hidden under a hood.

In a dark corner of the church Matilda bowed before me. I whispered, 'Tell me your sins, child.'

'My maid dropped my bread on the floor and I beat her,' she said. 'I was too hard. She was clumsy, not wicked. Forgive me, Father.'

'Tell me about the knight Sampson of Rouen — and remember you are in God's house, and God will strike you dead if you lie.'

She shook her head, lost. 'I know no man of that name.'

'He says you have plans to flee back to Flanders.'

She gave a harsh laugh. 'What nonsense, Father. I love my husband far too much. We have a family and will have many more. Why would I want to leave him?'

I threw back my hood and raised her from her knees. 'Of course you wouldn't,' I said and held her to me. 'What shall we do with the thief and liar Sampson?'

And Matilda told me. That very day he was tortured. Strips of skin were peeled off him till he was more blood than body. But while he still lived, each of his ankles and wrists were tied to a horse and the horses whipped and sent galloping to the corners of the earth.

Matilda's face was fierce but happy as she watched Sampson be torn apart.

'One day we shall do that to Harold Godwinson,' she laughed.

1064
HAROLD HOSTAGE

Matilda's dreams of England are close enough to breathe on. Edward is old and sick. Harold Godwinson — the Saxon who wants to be king — is in my power.

He was shipwrecked on the shores of France.

He lived but was made prisoner by my friend Guy of Ponthieu, and Guy sold him to me.

Harold and his little troop of guards were brought to me at Rouen.

I treated Godwinson like the great lord that he was in England. We went hunting together and he shared our feasts with entertainers in my halls at Rouen. Harold and his troop joined me on one of my raids into Brittany, we slept in the same tent, and I treated him like a brother.

After a month of this we returned to Rouen, to Matilda and our three sons and two daughters, with another child soon to be born. The feasts were huge with the animals we had hunted, and the wine was the best Harold would ever taste. But Matilda sulked.

When Harold arrived, she had cried, 'Kill him, William. Gouge out his eyes the way his father did to Alfred. Peel off his skin and have him torn apart by horses,' she said, and rubbed her tiny hands together in joy.

112

Taillefer and Theroulde looked gloomy, and Tally muttered, 'We can't do that, my lady. A great lord and knight like Duke William cannot murder a guest under his own roof.'

JUST ONE TEENSY WEENSY STAB!

Matilda looked at him with eyes as poisonous as a snake. 'Then I shall murder him, you cowardly jester. I have the knife.'

Theroulde spoke softly. 'Harold Godwinson is under your husband's care. If you want to rule England we must look after him. If Harold dies, then all of England will hate us. The struggle to win the land will be fought to the last field.'

I said nothing but I knew the old man was right. Matilda threw her knife in temper, and it stuck into the floor before she marched out. I did not see her again until after our child was born the next month — a girl we called Agatha.

Today Harold is leaving for England, loaded down with gifts from Normandy. But the gift he left behind was most precious of all. He left after promising that I, William of Normandy, would be the next king of England when Edward the Holy died. He swore over the bones of the saints in Bayeux Cathedral. No man breaks an oath like that.

Harold was a fine and handsome man, a great warrior and leader of men. Matilda made his image in a tapestry before she went sulking.

Harold had become a great friend by now. But is Harold Godwinson also a great liar? We shall see. I shall start to build an army of knights and foot soldiers. I shall fill a fortress with weapons and the coastal fields of Normandy with war horses. I shall build a fleet of strong ships to ride the fierce waves of the English Channel. I shall have my carpenters build the wooden walls of castles ready to carry over to England.

CONNECT CASTLE UPRIGHT (A), TO CASTLE CROSS-BEAM (B2)...

I shall land in England in peace. If Harold Godwinson is a liar, then I shall land at war. I shall kill him and he will deserve it.

Edward is a sickly man.

Soon, Matilda, soon.

1066
EDWARD'S END

Messengers arrived with the news we had been waiting for. 'Waiting for a dozen years,' Matilda snapped. Edward the holy man was dead. He died on 5 January in the year of Our Lord, 1066.

'When can I wear my crown?' my wife asked as she sat and made a tapestry of our story. She showed Harold swearing to make me king.

SWEAR!

CROSS MY HEART!

ADDED LATER

'I shall sail when the winter is over and it is safe,' I said.

'And Harold will take your throne while you sit and wait for the right wind, the right waves, the right boats.' She waved a finger under my nose. 'Harold will make himself king of England in one month, just wait and see.'

Matilda was right and Matilda was wrong. It did not take him a month. It took him one day. Tally brought me the news. 'Harold had himself crowned on 6 January,' he said. He looked at me. 'You should be angry, you look happy.'

'Oh, I am Taillefer, my clown, my singer, my friend. I am a man of war. I have fought all my life and war is my joy.'

'And Harold is a great fighter,' Theroulde put in. 'It will be like two giants of Troy – Hector against Achilles.'

117

I knew that story. 'And I am Achilles — the winner,' I laughed. 'If Matilda's dream is to wear the crown of England, then my dream is to fight and win it for her.'

'Like Roland,' Taillefer said with a nod. He plucked at his lute and sang.

LET US SING FOR MIGHTY ROLAND,
GREATEST KNIGHT IN ALL THE WORLD.
LET US SING FOR MIGHTY ROLAND,
GREATER MAN WAS NEVER BORN.

We had no wine, but we were drunk on happiness.

I wrote to Harold Godwinson to remind him he had sworn the crown of England would be mine. His sister was to marry my son, and he was to marry my daughter Adela. His reply made Matilda's blood boil like cooking oil.

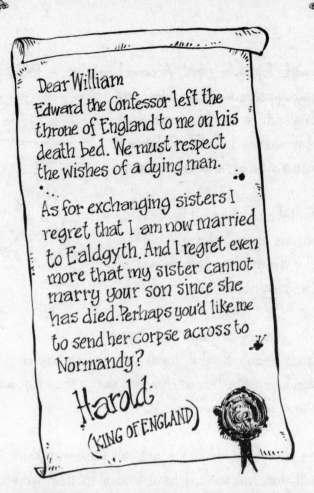

Dear William

Edward the Confessor left the throne of England to me on his death bed. We must respect the wishes of a dying man.

As for exchanging sisters I regret that I am now married to Ealdgyth. And I regret even more that my sister cannot marry your son since she has died. Perhaps you'd like me to send her corpse across to Normandy?

Harold
(KING OF ENGLAND)

It may take months to put my army and navy together but that is good. I am not the only lord preying on the English throne. Harold Godwinson has a brother, Tostig, a Viking warlord who hates Harold as only a brother can hate a brother.

119

I met Tostig in April. A comet had appeared in the skies over England. It was like a brilliant star with a tail. We all knew it was a sign of a great disaster.

SOME SAY A SIGN OF DISASTER!

Taillefer sighed. 'The trouble is no one knows who will suffer the disaster — the Vikings or the English or the Normans.'

My spies in England are saying Godwinson's English lords are telling him he should invade Normandy and put a stop to our plans, but he won't do it.

He says that when we set sail his great ships will just sink ours. I have a plan to deal with that. I said to the sour-smelling Tostig, 'If you attack him from the north then I'll attack from the south.'

'Why should I do that?' Tostig grunted. He was the most vile Viking of them all and smelled of dead cows from the leather shirt, breeches and cloaks he wore.

TOSTIG

'I will give you the North of England with its rich wheat fields and farms for your Viking friends,' I promised.

Matilda held her nose while we talked. When Tostig left she said, 'Harold will defeat Tostig.'

I shrugged. 'It doesn't matter. Harold's army and his ships will fly north to deal with Tostig.'

Old Theroulde agreed. 'Tostig will give him a hard battle and Harold Godwinson will lose

121

men and weapons. Tostig will make Harold weaker,' he said.

'But if Tostig wins you promised to give him the North of England,' Tally reminded me.

'I lied,' I said. Either way, William shall be the conqueror.

1066
FAMILY FEUDING

October. My armies are ready to sail. I need the right winds and weather. Storms have swept the seas for over a month. But today I was told the joyful news.

Harold has beaten his brother, Tostig, at a battle they are calling Stamford Bridge. Taillefer showed me the site on a map.

Norman traders have sailed the coasts of England for a hundred years and they tell me the beaches of the south are best for landing. Pevensey, they said, will make a good shore to aim for.

Matilda and Theroulde bent over the map. 'If we cross now then Harold will have to drag his army two hundred miles south to stop us,' Matilda said. 'They'll be too tired to fight. Go now, King William. Go while the storms have calmed down.'

I gathered my knights and told them Normandy would be under the care of Matilda and my son Richard. If we die in the battle, those lords must tell their sons to obey my wife.

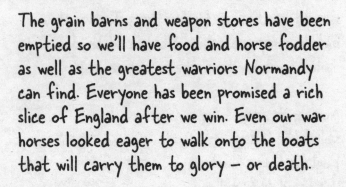

The grain barns and weapon stores have been emptied so we'll have food and horse fodder as well as the greatest warriors Normandy can find. Everyone has been promised a rich slice of England after we win. Even our war horses looked eager to walk onto the boats that will carry them to glory – or death.

This has been the year of storms. Each foul wind has driven us back. But storms never last.

Of course, Harold wanted to know about my plans, so he sent spies to find out about my armies on the shores. We captured the spies. 'Should we hang them?' Matilda asked.

But why? Instead, I told them, 'Go back to King Harold and tell him he might have saved himself the trouble of sending you spies. He'll soon learn my plans. Go and tell him from me that he can hide in the safest place he can find. I will track him down before the end of the year.'

Today I boarded my ship. It was Matilda's secret gift to me. My loving wife had bought this ship, the *Mora*, out of her own money. It is the finest in the fleet, with carved, painted and golden fittings. At the front — the bows — there is a golden figure of our youngest son, William. In his mouth, a trumpet made of ivory.

The storms are sinking like Harold's crown in a ditch. Look out Pevensey, the Normans are coming.

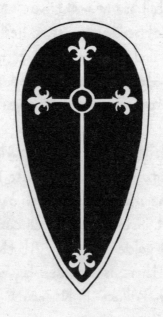

1066
LANDING AND LOSS

Do not ask me to tell you about the battle that we won. I was at the heart of it. If you wanted a map of a forest then you wouldn't ask someone who was in the middle of the thickest trees, would you? I can only tell what I saw. The historians will tell you what happened.

We had landed near a place called Hastings.

The first thing we did was to build a wooden castle there.

HELLOOOO!

We made sure our men were fed and rested. When Harold arrived, we were ready for him.

It was not an even battle. Harold had foot soldiers and a few archers. I had horse soldiers and whole troops of archers. He could not win. Yet, somehow, brave Harold and his little army held out from dawn till dusk but we finally drove them from the battlefield.

Of course, they sat at the top of a hill the English called Senlac. I knew as well as any warrior that to attack uphill is nearly impossible. Swords and battleaxes and spears are raining DOWN on you and your horses.

Harold Godwinson – or 'King' Harold as he called himself – stood there like a rock. Even at a thousand paces I could sense him mocking me. 'You came to fight, William? So, fight.'

TWIRL! TWIRL!

'We have horses,' I cried to my knights. 'Let's ride at them and drive them off their hill.'

And what did my lords do? They sat there. No one wanted to take the lead. 'What's wrong with them?' I moaned to Taillefer.

Tally spoke loudly. 'Duke William, only a fool would attack those brave English on their hilltop. Where will you find such a fool, my lord? I am your fool. I shall lead the charge.'

He turned to the knights who shuffled in their saddles and looked down, ashamed, at the ground. 'Will you all follow me?'

My old friend pulled his sword from its scabbard and threw it high in the air. He caught it cleanly, pulled out his dagger and threw that up too. Then he sent them both soaring into the air and juggled them in a blaze of sun–glittering steel. He spurred his horse forward. 'For William and Matilda. Will you betray your lord and the lovely lady Matilda? Make her a queen.'

I knew how much Matilda hated Taillefer, so it was princely of him to name her. My knights loved my Matilda as much as I did. They put aside their fears and drew their swords. But by then Tally was fifty paces ahead of them and starting to climb Senlac Hill.

Harold had few horsemen but four of them raced down the hill towards the brave and foolish Taillefer. He was still juggling his sword and dagger when they reached him and cut him down. He was dead before his flying sword hit the ground.

I felt a rage boiling inside me, but so did my knights. They galloped fearlessly towards the enemy, screaming their anger.

Arrows began to rain down and my archers replied with a deadly rain on the heads of the English. I moved forward, past the body of Tally the fool, and ordered men to carry his body back to the boats.

For hours we battled up the hill and were driven back till we were close to exhausted. We stopped, as men do in long battles, and ate bread and drank wine. I called to my brother Odo, 'How do we shift them from the hill?'

He shook his head. That was when I had the ghost of Taillefer in my head whispering, 'Run away. Remember Arques Castle? Run away and they will follow.'

I shivered and muttered a thanks to Tally. Then I gave the order. 'Next time we attack, pretend to turn your backs on them. Lead the English down the hill. Odo's knights will be waiting for them in that clump of trees.'

And that was what we did. And, just as Taillefer had promised, it worked quite wonderfully. The bravest and best of the English charged down after my men like fish after bait, and the hook was waiting for them once they were on the flat and blood-slicked fields. Odo's horses came from the woods and his knights butchered the cream of the English warriors.

Odo cried with joy. 'Now send arrows high into the air so their shields will be lifted, and we can charge at them again.

The long day was coming to an end and the sun was setting. The sky grew dark as a wall of arrows rose into the clouds and fell like death onto Harold's guard.

I watched my tired knights on weary horses make one last charge and chop down Harold. When the English saw their leader fall – their leader, not their king – then they stumbled from the battlefield and fled for their lives.

The battle was over. The killing went on as it always does. English women swarmed over Senlac Hill to find their men to bury. Or they simply stripped the corpses to sell the weapons and armour. I was too tired to care.

'We won, brother,' Odo said.

But my joy was small. The prize was great. England. The price was great too. Poor, dear Tally.

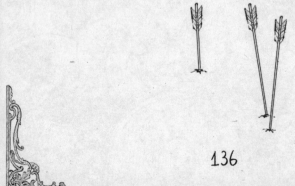

1067
REBELS AND REVENGE

After the coronation I found out how hard it is to rule two countries — Normandy and England — with miles of ocean in between. Matilda is in charge of Normandy and Maine while I send my knights across England to take over my new kingdom.

Matilda was happy to be a queen in Normandy. Once England is safe she will come across and be crowned. That will be her dream made real. She didn't care that I lost my friend Taillefer. She even wrote to let me know old Theroulde had died.

My KING william

What a thrill it is to write that word, <u>KING</u>. Normandy is safe in my little hands. Any trouble has been crushed by the brave army of trusted men you left at home. Old Theroulde died on horseback. He was riding out to deal with some outlaws near Falaise when he dropped off his horse. I'm sure you'll miss him, but I don't need him to help me rule.

Our sons are being taught by the Italian Lanfranc, and the girls are learning Latin at the abbey in Caen. The nuns are strict, and the girls hate them. But they will grow up to marry great princes, and rule like me. They need to be able to read and write so they must suffer the cold abbey rooms and the dreadful food. I did when I was their age.

I am planning my trip to England to join you and have that crown put on my lovely head. You said in your last letter that Taillefer died to make me queen. Thank you Taillefer. I never liked you. You are no great loss. You were just a palace juggler, jester and singer. I am a queen.

I shall see you later this year, my king.

Your faithful queen Matilda
xXx

My queen will come from peaceful Normandy to dangerous England. It seems she wants to feel the danger for herself.

Of course, some English chiefs tried to lead their people to rebel. I showed my lords what to do when they reached the land they had won.

'We build castles,' I said. 'We build them high. We build them fast. The English peasants and their war chiefs will look up at them and see them as a sign of our power. A keep on top of a mound of earth – a motte – and the buildings my soldiers need below – a bailey.' I drew a sketch to show them what I meant. The English peasants – the losers – can sweat to raise those castles. One day we will make them out of stone.

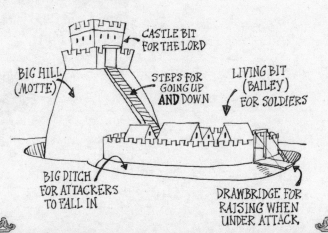

CASTLE BIT FOR THE LORD

BIG HILL (MOTTE)

STEPS FOR GOING UP **AND** DOWN

LIVING BIT (BAILEY) FOR SOLDIERS

BIG DITCH FOR ATTACKERS TO FALL IN

DRAWBRIDGE FOR RAISING WHEN UNDER ATTACK

THAT'S the way to conquer a land. The other way is to beat and crush and punish the rebels. Matilda wants to help me. When she arrives in England, we'll set off to the rebel area in the North of England. Those foolish English in the North do not understand they are beaten, that they are under Norman rule. That they must obey.

They will understand better when they are dead in the fields.

1068
ENDING ENGLAND

This year we crowned Matilda, Queen of England. The English called the royal women 'wife of the king'. They hated it when I had her crowned Queen of England.

Like sailors on our warships, Matilda and I work together like a crew. There are rebels in the North? Then together we will march to defeat them.

My lords took most of the lands from the English lords. But some of them said they'd be true to me. English warriors like Copsi swore to rule the North as a true Norman. What did the English do? They waited just five weeks before they trapped him inside a church. Then they set it on fire.

As Copsi ran out they were waiting, and they sliced his head from his body.

At first, I sent my trusty Robert Cumyn into the English city of Durham. A monk's report came back to me.

W

When the people of Durham heard Cumyn was on his way they planned to escape. But a fierce snowstorm and a hard frost stopped them. Then they decided instead to either murder the Earl ... or die. The bishop of Durham warned the Earl and told him to stay away from Durham. Cumyn ignored him and entered Durham with seven hundred men, planning to punish the rebels. The people suffered and any man who raised a weapon against a Norman was cut down.

Then, very early in the morning of 31 January, the rebels broke in through all the gates. They ran through the city, hither and thither, they killed the earl's men. So many were killed that every street was covered in blood and filled with Norman bodies. The blood that flowed in the streets was frozen by the bitter January winds.

The earl himself held out in a house near Palace Green so the rebels set it on fire. The flaming sparks flying upwards caught the western tower of the cathedral. The people knelt down and begged St Cuthbert to save his church from burning; and immediately a wind arose from the east which drove the flames backwards from the church.

The earl's house continued to blaze. Some of the people inside were burnt, some were slaughtered as soon as they stepped outside. The earl was put to death along with all of his followers, except for one, who escaped wounded and told the dreadful story.

Matilda heard the news and shrugged. 'If the English want to be hard then let's show them the Normans can be harder.'

Her idea was firstly to starve the people of the North till they were too weak to fight. We didn't just want to defeat the North — we wanted to destroy it. Every building our soldiers came across was burned. Every animal was killed so there was nothing left for the people to eat except their horses, dogs and cats.

We ordered that crops, farm animals, tools and food be burned to ashes. More than 100,000 people died starving. Disease came along to add to the misery of the ones who were left.

Every man and boy we found was hacked to death — their corpses were left to rot by the side of the roads. The starving survivors were so desperate they ate the corpses to stay alive.

They call our ruthless revenge 'The Harrying of the North'. It was simply a lesson to the English people who wanted to rebel.

The North was like a desert. The towns and villages will struggle to recover in twenty years' time. The North certainly didn't revolt again. Cruel? Don't call me cruel. The English started it.

1077
FAMILY AND FALL

I have ruled England for ten years. My lords have built their castles and the English are mostly our slaves.

Our priests have built huge churches – cathedrals. We say they are the houses of God. The truth is they are just like my castles and make the English see what power we have. Castles like my Tower of London stand as a sign that the forces of the world are on my side.

TOWER OF LONDON

The cathedrals are a sign that even God is on my side.

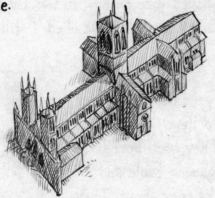

Like God I hold the power of the world in my hand. I should be content. But troubles — like arrows at Hastings — fall from the skies when you don't expect them.

I know the English hate me. Let them. But my own son Robert hates me. That is sharper than a snake's bite.

My Robert has always been lazy and weak. Greedy too. When Matilda joined me in England, I made him duke of Normandy. I visited him there.

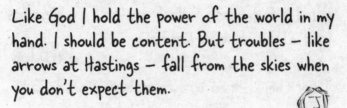

ROBERT
(THE SULK!)

Two of my other sons — William and Henry — played a wicked joke on him. It was the sort of joke Taillefer would have liked. I still miss Taillefer.

When we were back in Rouen, William and Henry played dice with Robert. They grew bored. They left the gaming table and crept onto the balcony above. They filled a toilet pot full of pee (and other stinking matter).

A WEE JOKE!

They then tipped it over Robert's head. Tally would have laughed. Robert didn't.

He flew into such a rage he attacked his brothers. I had to come between them. Robert cried like a baby that I should punish them. I didn't.

His revenge was foul as that toilet pot. He tried to attack my castle at Rouen. When I fought back, he ran off to Matilda's brother

148

– his uncle – in Flanders. From there he went to war – attacking Normandy.

I joined the battle against him and met him face to face. To my shame he knocked me off my horse and raised his sword to kill me.

When I cried out, he knew his father's face was under the helmet and he spared my life. I sometimes wish he'd killed me before the next bite of the snake.

Robert was short of money to pay his army. Then I heard he found money to keep up the

battle against me. Where did the money come from?

Oh, the shame, the bitter taste of it. The money came from his mother — my Matilda.

If I cannot trust Matilda, then I can trust no one.

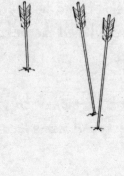

1083
MATILDA MOURNED

Matilda has always said I should forgive our rebel son, Robert. And so, I have. I have found a son again.

But today I lost a wife. Matilda died. I was by her bedside as she lay in painful sleep. I held her hand till at last her breathing stopped.

Tally would have sung his song of Roland over her cold body and so I muttered it instead of a prayer.

> *For Roland let our salt tears flow.*
> *Let us sing for mighty Roland,*
> *Greatest knight in all the world.*
> *Let us sing for mighty Roland,*
> *Greater man was never born.*

Greater woman was never born.

She was the mother of our four sons and six daughters. She loved them all — even the foolish Robert. I know she loved the weakling more than me. It doesn't matter now.

I shall battle on. I have my enemies. I must face them alone.

Goodnight, Matilda. We'll meet again in some better place.

1087
REGRETS AND ENDINGS

The priests are gathering round me like brown, hooded crows waiting to feast on a dying lamb in a February field. My doctors say I will get better but they are lying to me.

The priests will hear me tell them all my sins before I die. They will forgive me so I can enter the kingdom of Heaven with a clean soul.

I'll be with you soon, Matilda. I was such a strong man. But after you died, I drank the wines of France and ate the greasy deer of England, the rich loaves of Normandy and the strong cheeses of Maine. What else was there to do? I have grown fat.

The strongest horse was needed to carry me. I had given up hunting but still had to appear on the battlefields of Normandy and England. My soldiers needed to see me if they were going to fight for me.

So, I rode out to Mantes when we attacked that great city.

I had the town burned to the ground and my horse was frightened by the shower of sparks.

My horse stumbled, and I slammed my stomach against the front of my saddle. I knew when I did it, I had burst my fat gut.

oOOOF!

That was five weeks ago, and I have suffered in agony. If death comes now, it will come as a welcome friend.

It won't be long now. I have handed my crown and sword to my son William Rufus. All I need to do now is to confess to the hooded-crow priests.

Of all the cruel things I did, there is one that haunts me. The attack they call the Harrying of the North. So many dead, so many who died slowly. They didn't die bravely in battle like dear Taillefer, they didn't die swiftly like Harold.

I do not blame myself for Harold's death. It was how he would want to die. I am not sorry for the deaths of the traitors who tried to kill me.

But those English peasants in the North. They died slowly and miserably. I am sorry.

There, priests. I have said it. Forgive me. Pray for me. I am tired now. Let me rest.

Goodnight, my sons and daughters. Good morning, Taillefer, Theroulde and Matilda.

END

INDEX

Alan of Brittany (Norman duke) 67
Alfred (William's cousin) 45–6, 49, 53–5, 57, 69, 104, 112
ambushes 31, 76, 78
archers 72, 128, 132
armour 38, 76–8, 82, 96, 136
arrows 38, 79, 99, 132–3, 135, 147

battle-axes 76, 107, 128
battles, brutal 14, 39–41, 62, 64, 81–3, 104, 121, 123–4, 127–8, 132, 136, 149–50, 152, 154–5
bishops 15–16, 18, 143
blood 10–11, 40, 64, 110, 118, 133, 143

caltrops (ground spikes) 79
castles, crucial 19, 31, 48, 67–77, 89, 91, 96, 101, 107, 115, 128, 132, 139, 146, 148
cathedrals 114, 143, 146–7
Charles III (king of France) 28–9
Cnut (king of England) 35, 41, 44–7, 49, 53–4, 57, 104
comets 120
Copsi (English warrior) 141–2
corpses 13, 119, 136, 144
crowns, and crownings 9, 14–16, 55, 102, 116–18, 126, 137–8, 141, 155
cruelty 9, 11, 44, 56–7, 82–3, 85, 92, 145, 155
Cumyn, Robert (Norman noble) 142–3

daggers 48, 62–3, 130–1
dogs 9, 34, 57, 67, 98–9, 144

ears, cut off 44, 49, 56
Edward the Confessor (king of England) 14, 45–6, 49, 53, 56, 66, 69, 102–5, 111, 114–16, 119
Emma (William's aunt/queen of England) 33, 35–6, 40, 45, 47–53, 55–6, 69, 89, 102–5
Ethelred (king of England) 34–5, 40–1, 44–5, 47, 104
Eva (William's sister) 9–10, 13–16, 18, 20
eyes, put out 55, 57, 104, 112

feasts 37–8, 63, 99–100, 112, 153
feet, cut off 56, 84
fires 17–18, 98, 101, 142–3

Gilbert of Brionne (Norman noble) 67
Godwin (English earl) 54–6, 102–3
gold 14, 40, 60, 72, 106, 125
Guy of Ponthieu (William's friend) 111

hands, cut off 56, 84
Harold Godwinson (king of England) 103–4, 111–26, 128–9, 131, 133, 136, 155
Harold Harefoot (king of England) 54, 69
Harrying of the North 144–5, 155
Henry (king of France) 39, 66, 68, 70–3, 75–9

horses, hoards of 55, 59, 77, 79, 81–2, 90–1, 96, 100–1, 110, 112, 115, 124, 128–31, 133, 136, 138, 144, 149, 154
hunting 9, 98–9, 112, 154

javelins (weapons) 38, 79
Jerusalem 39, 50, 59–61
jewels 96, 101, 106
jokes 9, 13, 15, 44, 46, 58, 86, 148
juggling 39, 63, 130–1

lances (weapons) 31–2, 76
languages 15–17, 97, 138
leather 12–13, 84, 121

maps 50, 76, 123–4, 127
Matilda of Flanders (William's wife/queen of England) 86–111, 116–18, 121, 125, 130–1, 137–41, 144, 147–8, 150–3, 156
monasteries 10, 34, 55, 66, 81
monks 18, 20–5, 30, 34, 46, 53, 55, 66, 81, 108, 142
Mundi (William's teacher) 22–3, 25–6, 28, 30, 33, 66, 81

Normandy, dukes of 10, 27–39, 49, 58–61, 63–5, 91, 93, 102, 114, 147
Normans, nasty 8, 14, 16–19, 123, 126, 140–4, 160
noses, cut off 44, 49, 56
nuns 9, 11, 13–16, 18, 20, 104, 106, 108, 138

oaths, swearing 114, 116, 118
Odo (William's brother) 132–3, 136
Orderic Vitalis (English monk) 18
Osbern (William's servant) 68

parchments, piles of 11–12, 46, 53, 76
peasants, pitiful 12, 16, 68, 84, 90, 92, 94–5, 99, 139, 155
pee, pouring 148
pikes (weapons) 76, 80
pilgrims 39, 59–60
poison 38, 59, 67, 106
pretence, tactical 79–80, 87–8, 132–3
prisoners 57, 74, 84, 104, 111

rebels 19, 31, 56, 65–7, 75, 83, 95, 137–45, 151
revenge 25, 71, 137, 145, 148
Richard I (duke of Normandy) 27, 32–3
Richard II (duke of Normandy) 27, 33–6
Richard III (William's uncle/duke of Normandy) 27, 36–8
Robert I (William's father/duke of Normandy) 21, 27, 37–9, 47, 49–51, 57–62, 64–7, 102
Robert (William's son/duke of Normandy) 102, 138, 147–52
Rollo (duke of Normandy) 27–30
rules 99–101
running away 74, 79–80, 84, 132–3

Sampson of Rouen (Norman knight) 107–10
Saxons, suffering 14–17, 19, 40, 111
ships 40, 51, 102, 115, 117, 120–1, 124, 132
sieges 72–5, 83–4
skin, stripping off 110, 112
slaves 61, 146
spears 38, 79, 128
spies 72, 120, 124–5
starvation 31, 83, 144

swords 22, 38, 40, 47, 81, 107, 128, 130-1, 149, 155

Taillefer (William's jester) 40, 46, 53, 56-8, 103-4
    advice of 44, 57, 61-2, 75-6, 79, 86, 106-8, 113, 117, 120, 122-3, 129, 133
    as bodyguard 72, 82-4
    death of 131-2, 136-8, 148, 155-6
    and Matilda 88-9, 91-4, 97-8
    as singer 39, 48-9, 63-4, 70, 118, 151
tanners 12, 91
tapestries 48, 89, 95, 97, 114, 116
Theroulde (William's trainer) 64-5, 68, 97, 106, 108
    advice of 70-2, 75-8, 87-9, 93-4, 113, 117, 121, 124
    death of 137-8, 156
    lessons of 38-9, 41, 44-7, 50, 56-7
torture, terrifying 56, 110
Tostig (Harold Godwinson's brother) 119-21, 123

Tower of London 19, 146
Turchetil (William's cousin) 68

Vikings, vicious 10, 19, 28, 30-3, 40-52, 119-21

Walter (William's bodyguard) 68
William the Conqueror (king of England) 6-11, 14-20
    early life of 21-5
    enemies of 53-8, 61-87, 111-22, 137-45
    fall of 146-50
    family of 12-13, 23-52, 58-65, 84-113, 116-18, 121-7, 130-1, 137, 140-1, 144-53, 156
    and Harold 103-4, 111-36, 155
    marriage of 87-111
William Longsword (duke of Normandy) 27, 31-2
William Rufus (William's son/king of England) 125, 138, 148, 155

NORMANS
RULE
OK!